BRILLIANCE, SPILLING

BRILLIANCE,
Spilling

Twenty Years
of Perugia Press Poetry

perugia
PRESS

Florence, Massachusetts
1997–2016

Perugia Press publishes one collection of poetry each year, by a woman at the beginning of her publishing career. Our mission is to produce beautiful books that interest long-time readers of poetry and welcome those new to poetry. We also aim to celebrate and promote poetry whenever we can, and to keep the cultural discussion of poetry inclusive.

Perugia Press extends deeply felt thanks to the many individuals who have contributed to the press over the years. To make a tax-deductible donation, please contact us directly or visit our website. Perugia Press is a tax-exempt, nonprofit 501(c)(3) corporation.

Book design by Susan Kan, Rebecca Olander, and Jeff Potter

Cover art is "June nights, I slip in and out of the moon," acrylic, 19" x 19", by Scout Cuomo. Used with permission of the artist (scoutcuomo.com).

Each poet has granted permission to reprint her poem from her Perugia Press book. Before being published by Perugia Press, several of these poems first appeared in literary journals: "A Sorceress Strolls New Grass" in *Cider Press Review;* "In Flight" in *Barrow Street* (with a different title); "I Don't Want to Say How Lost I've Been" in *Poetry East;* "Kore" in *Poetry;* "Migration" in *Alligator Juniper;* "Custodian" in *Calyx;* "Bogles Wharf" in *Ellipses;* "What Her Father Cast" in *North American Review;* "The mountaintop as an opening and an opening" in *Country Dog Review;* "The Ewe Lamb" in *Harvard Divinity Bulletin;* "Jewelweed" in *Folio;* "Where the Sentence Ends the Sentiment Burgeons" in *Shenandoah;* "Reddening the Moon" in *Bellingham Review;* and "The City That Care Forgot" in *North American Review.*

Library of Congress Cataloging-in-Publication Data

Title: Brilliance, spilling : twenty years of Perugia Press poetry, 1997-2016.
Description: Florence, Massachusetts : Perugia Press, [2016]
Identifiers: LCCN 2016035764 | ISBN 9780997807608 (pbk. : alk. paper)
Subjects: LCSH: American poetry--21st century. | American poetry--20th
  century.
Classification: LCC PS617 .B75 2016 | DDC 811/.608--dc23
LC record available at https://lccn.loc.gov/2016035764

Perugia Press
PO Box 60364
Florence, MA 01062
editor@perugiapress.com
perugiapress.org
perugiapress.com

for Susan Kan

Contents

Lynne Thompson

A SORCERESS STROLLS NEW GRASS

I am neither mother nor turquoise neckwear
but you are such young women,
such new potatoes, and there is much
for me to tell you:

> that bishops joyride in the dead of night,
> that blue's favorite color is blue
> and earth is just a gaudy paragraph.

And though I am ripe as November, I can tell you

> no sorceress ever abandons midday
> and a sculptor is always better
> in a waterbed.

Of course, I'm vainglorious with my knowing and croaking—

but you women are writing your own Book of Migration
and without warning, I feel useless as an empty valise.
What you know makes the bandicoot fly and you converse
in flamingo and seashell, smell like smoke and rapscallions.

> You are tambourines
> in the stewing pot,
> a crucible of cymbals.

> Being fresh as new grass, you
> inspire me to astonish, then gloat;
> to beg no pardon, then begin.

In Flight

The Himalayan legend says
there are beautiful white birds
that live completely in flight.
They are born in the air,

must learn to fly before falling
and die also in their flying.
Maybe you have been born
into such a life

with the bottom dropping out.
Maybe gravity is claiming you
and you feel
ghost-scripted.

For the one who lives inside the fall,
the sky beneath the sky of all.

Gail Martin

I Don't Want to Say How Lost I've Been

Missed my road by Cathead Point, took the wrong loop on the trail at Port Oneida. Got so turned around on Voice Road by North Bar Lake I couldn't speak for three days. I went to the IGA after it closed. Good Harbor Grill doesn't serve dinner. I never know which side of the road the river will be on. It takes me a while to realize I'm lost. You could call that confidence or part of the problem. Lake = north, lake = north, I say to myself, but lake = west and northwest a bit down the road, and there's a lake to the east here too. A friend's husband draws a map by hand each time she leaves, CANADA at the top, MEXICO at the bottom. The oceans are implied. This is to help her know if she overshoots a turn. I understand. I love maps, the names, the blue shapes of lakes and rivers. I can find my way anywhere theoretically. What's hard is the YOU ARE HERE part. And it isn't exactly loneliness, although I'm calling it that.

Carol Edelstein

ONE SUMMER DAY BEFORE WE MET

Bicycling through a heat wave,
I stopped to browse under the shady tent
of the library's annual lawn sale.
Folded into an animal husbandry textbook
between pages that explained in pictures
the digestive system of the bovine quadruped (cow),
notable for the number of stomachs (four)

required for her grass to become flesh,
I found an embossed invitation
requesting my (the receiver's) presence
at a wedding reception long over.
I love how our minds
can bring such a party to life,
can pour the radiant heat

and salt breeze of this real morning
around imagined strangers,
remarkable likenesses of the actual
congregation of people who know us
yet who from a distance might sound
like doves, or gravel
shaken through a sieve.

Isn't happiness always one part
regret to two parts sky?
I slipped that invitation
into my pocket, slid the book
back onto the table, took up
my bike, and pedaled on,
legs pumping *find me, find me.*

Faye George

KORE

Flowers drew me forth
that time when I went out
and the ground beneath my feet
fell away.

I held on to the stems
as the dark pulled me in,
held on as if I clutched
the light of the world in my hand,
not the torn throats
of narcissus blooms.

Through the long night
in the iron earth
I clung to the fickleness
of beauty, the only candle
for the tomb.

Melody S. Gee

MIGRATION

After the rain, trees burn with monarchs,
come this winter on dust-and-paper bodies.
Some of the dead cling to trash on the road,

frames of wings like frames of broken windows.
You say you never saw anything like them
in China, though you cannot say for sure.

As a girl, you leashed crickets with ox hairs
and baited bees with sweet tomato flesh.
But nothing like this, you say, *like this orange.*

This monarch generation lives three times
longer than its parents, than it would without
a migration to complete. They are given

time to break their bodies over mountains
and heave themselves onto warm trees
so they all might survive. Are you wondering

how much more time you have been given
to learn a language and forget a language, to break
your body over an ocean for this pale

redwood dusk and this daughter?
I know you were not drawn here to save
yourself. I cannot tell you that I have

nothing to save, nothing that waits for me
to be drawn, nothing that says, *you must,*
you must break your wings for this.

Gail Thomas

CUSTODIAN
for William Zimmerman

The man who loved flowers
walked every morning to
PS 128 where he mopped
vomit from the lunchroom,
scrubbed toilets and
collared boys who spit
in water fountains.
He was proud of the shine
on the gym floor,
his honest work.

At home in the narrow yard
he knelt to fertilize
tired city dirt,
coaxing bulbs that would
give themselves
to sooty air in masses
of brilliance, spilling
over the wire fence.
Under the moon
he walked with his wife,
breathing a litany
of iris, rose,
snow-on-the-mountain,
gloriosa daisy, bleeding heart.
Later, when his legs
and eyes stopped working,
when she shrank and shook,
the house was sold.
From the fifth floor

of a high-rise he dreamed
of fringed petals,
slow openings, yellow pollen
dusting his fingertips.
When he woke, he lifted
her pale limbs, changed
urine sheets and bathed
the soft folds of her body
in rose water.

Almitra David

BOGLES WHARF

BOGLES WHARF

we stand here at the
edge   cast
our lines into the
bay   not far from the
pier   not far from the
piling where an
osprey's nest still
holds to the top

in this sanctuary
wild swans and herons
gather   the sun burns
from orange to red then
disappears   leaving
our faces suddenly gray
and the geese a pale
black in the unlit sky

this is when we
remember everything

the first fresh
Susquehanna water   the
mingling with
Atlantic salt   the
layers   one upon the other
of gifts   as though
Gaea herself had laid in
stores for eons of feasts

now   a few
watermen dock in the slips
take stock of the crab and
oyster catch   consider the
size of the rockfish
they used to know the
predator   the quiet shadow
of a hawk's wing   the

fast splash of talons   we
reel in our lines   move
closer together   touch
shoulders as if to
brace ourselves   the
water still moves with
the tides as though
nothing has changed

Jenifer Browne Lawrence

WHAT HER FATHER CAST

He said stand on your own
two feet and her shadow
swam into a fish
spooled from her reel
at the speed of grayling

He spoke the river's name
Tonsina   shade of a salmon's breath
flaring in the grizzly's mouth

She took off her clothes
to hang from the side of the boat
her legs refused
to fuse into a tail
as planned

Kneel at the river's edge
if the father you love
has been drinking
again   cling

as sea lice
cling to a salmon after death
then fall to the fire
when the fish is cooked through

There goes her shadow again
There goes the reel

Lisa Allen Ortiz

PATOIS

When she spoke, birds came out her mouth,
every word a different species. Thus the civic sorrow
of mass extinction became for her a personal affront—
her vocabulary contracted by 200 feathered words a day.

Her dictionary: *A Guide to Birds*—glossy plates, antique precision,
aquatints of wings and eyes—all of it so out of date. By then we typed.
In the end, she uttered a few remaining jays and doves.
She stuttered strings of starlings, cawed a garbage bird or two—

then grew quiet as a tree, sighed a final pair of finches.
She died, her mouth ajar and nestless. We texted our regrets.
We pen-scratched bits on paper and threw them toward her grave.
The air was empty, the grass and branches cheerless ash.

We felt sorry then. We wanted at least a flock of chimney swifts
to empty out her skull, rise mute and furious toward the moon.

Ida Stewart

THE MOUNTAINTOP AS AN OPENING
AND AN OPENING

See a phonograph,
       phonographic blossom—

     see music or pollen

in the wind;
or feel me—two hands directing a whisper,
warm, to your ear: either way

the impression is transmission
through and through.

     I see you

looking down into the crater, the unsound

earth.   I'm open like opening night.
Like the overture.   I'm a hearth to your hands.

I'm a deafness—

       What are the words?

I'm just a woman saying
listen here, listen here, listen here.

Diane Gilliam

MILK

Mama always said, You can't feed a baby
if there's no happiness in the milk. Now, we
didn't judge a man by what he had, but
by whether he took his pay home
before he went to the bar, and Burns Cantrell
did not. And he hit Meardie, which wasn't
no fault of hers, Mama said. So when she
had a baby come in strike time, Mama
bought two tins of canned milk out of
the dollar a week the company store
allowed each family for food, and sent me
to set them on Cantrells' porch every Monday
after Burns had went up the hill. Now,
it was the law among the miners that, come
a roof fall, you run. Everybody knowed
that was how it was. If you stop and look back
to see who's dead or trapped, you
only make more dead. Four days after the men
went back in, there come a bad roof fall, killed
sixteen. Daddy was back behind. Right off
the rocks broke one backbone and his jaw
in five places. Burns Cantrell was up front.
He heard them rocks begin to fall, and he run
back into the hole, pitch black, the mountain
crumbling like the end of the world,
and carried Daddy out. He knowed
he owed my mama for the milk.

Frannie Lindsay

THE EWE LAMB
—2 Samuel 12:3

I raised my one ewe lamb
as a daughter, fed her
red clover, the last hearts
of my cabbage, offered
her inky lips my cup.
She rested her chin
on my neck at night, her hoofs
on my cloak, her breathing
the wind on the waves
of sleep's pure waters.
Sleep: an animal's word
for *bless:* hoof of her heart
to the hoof of my heart.
The dusk before her slaughter
we walked together, pauper
and kin, over the meadow.
I sang to her, then
I unstrung the rusted bell
from her collar.

Nancy K. Pearson

JEWELWEED

Trajectories blast off,
arc and down a hundred times a day.
Oddments of seedpods, the neap tide of wind,
the recurved tails of jewelweed everywhere.

It was a Tuesday. I was drinking vodka
before noon. Outside the heat was a thorn,
the porch shade nervous, the remains of the lilies—
pitchforks.

Days started like this:
You couldn't find a sock to wear with your suit.
I couldn't find it for you. I couldn't hold a job.

A gnat suspended the breeze and arced for my glass.
I thought of all my landings, my fight with medium,
my quick ignitions and even faster snuffs.

The sun makes a beeline for my ice.
I pour another. I used to have a seedcase of dreams—
sainthood, the Olympics, an honest answer,
folded laundry.

When ripe, a pod of jewelweed explodes
under the slightest disturbance.
Trap one in your fingertips,
unzip.

Melanie Braverman

TELL

Let's talk
about sex, let's talk about what
you like to do, or have
done to you, or do to
yourself while someone else
is watching, say
you like it in cars, while you're
driving, maybe, his hands or her
mouth between your legs, or in
a basement, quiet except
for the sound of your
breathing, which is
getting
faster, you
can't
help it, you like
the way the air fits your skin like another
skin, the air and her breath or just
her breath, you can't tell
anymore but you like
it, you do, you're a little
scared even though you've done
this with him before, you've known
him for years, or maybe you
just met, at a bar, in the library, on
the street in the fog, walking
the pier at two A.M., admiring the boats, the birds
quiet
mostly, the aqua the red
beam from the light

house pulsing so you feel
your blood the way
it wants you to feel
it, you see
that man walking just
ahead of you, the woman
whose arms are swinging at, you
swear, the same
cadence as your own, my god, she
has an amazing ass, it's round or
small, whatever
kind of ass you like that's
it, moving in front
of you like a beacon, like
an offering, forget
every bad thing that ever
happened to you, forget
danger, have faith
in your own safety now, speed
up and tell
that man hello, he wants
you to, maybe
you like it at home, in your own
bed or at his house, the way someone
else's sheets feel like little
revelations across your back when she lifts
your shirt off and you
finally lie
down, after all
that kissing, your faces

rife with it, his
breath
and his rough
cheek or her
cheek smooth as sin there, her foreign
breath, or maybe she's so
familiar her breath
has come
to smell
like your own, you've fallen into bed exhausted
with the one you love and still something
in you stirs, your body rises
now, as if sex with this
person has become
part of your dream
life, talk
about that, the mysterious, the absolute
way you fall in-
to or out
of yourself, toward
another, toward that orange
place where anything
can happen or will and know
you'll
like it.

Corrie Williamson

WHERE THE SENTENCE ENDS
THE SENTIMENT BURGEONS

Years since the old woman's grandson turned
early to ash and years since she's seen the young
woman who was his lover but seeing her now
extends her arms crying you look just the same
as that first day coming up the driveway I saw you
forking hay from a feedtrough as the chaff
drifted in the sun and in the long wild loops
of your hair waving and laughing as if I knew you
already and him leaning on the pitchfork and smiling
the black seed of his dying already planted between
his hips brittle and black as a walnut smiling
as if he'd live forever or perhaps as if he knew
but it was all right because that night he would lie
by the young woman below the grandparents'
bedroom with the windows wide and know the yard
gonged with the deep blue temple bells of hyacinth
that the cows sucked moisture from the dark and the owl
in the barn laid her eggs slowly through the night's
course so that the hatchlings would feed
on one another and the girl's hair was a great
mystery flowing over him to mix with his
young man's beard red as falu paint on a Swedish
cottage or red as the tongue of the bowsprit
his brother will invoke not long from now wishing
to launch the body out to sea burning and red
as the ruff of twin foxes who bark and snarl
chasing each other through alfalfa rows until
they both roll showing the golden scythe
of their bellies to the moon and she shows them hers.

Linda Tomol Pennisi

REDDENING THE MOON
for Effie

On the balcony, with the moon
stuck to her shoulder. No.
On the balcony, with the moon
blooming from her mouth.
And her red shoes doing what—
dancing? And her red shoes
reddening the moon's blueness,
like her red shawl whitens her breasts
as they gleam there in Chicago,
October, early '70s, and almost thirty
years later when asked, *What*
does the moon remind you of?
my friend remembers this: her friend's
flesh, the photographer's flash,
and the moon low and sultry,
rounding its way to a glossy page
in Spain, the shoes high-heeled
and highlighted, her friend's
body a river shimmering
from shoes to moon, moon to shoes,
the dark that night vivid
and lipstick lush. And though tonight
as we walk this wide circle
atop this wide hill, the moon
so full we feel it pulls us
to the world's rim, we know the dark
may never be that lush again,
but our faces glow a little
and our pace slows as if our feet
have stepped into the color
most worth remembering.

Amanda Auchter

THE CITY THAT CARE FORGOT
You were here once; you will be here again. —Joanna Klink

What brings you back is the sugared air

that seeps its way through
the streets. The scrolled iron balconies,
banana-leaved courtyards, gas lamps draped

with bright plastic beads. Not the water-

stained drywall, crushed fence, the X-
marked houses. Not the ruin
of mosquito fever, flood, the history

of bodies hung by the neck in trees,
but how the river collects daylight, the sound

of trumpets in late afternoon. You return to this

humid sweep, the second lines of handkerchiefs,
magnolia in every scene. Long ago,
this was the city that care forgot: mold-scarred,

splintered chairs washing upstream. A city
of tents, of wind-wrapped shutters, shotgun

houses. What brings you back. The city

turns its umbrellas in the sun, lights fire
for roux. What calls you: the music

of a gate opening onto Tchoupitoulas Street,
chicory-heat, the roof tiles

in the black sky. The water. The rising.

Catherine Anderson

THE LIFE OF WOOD
Angkor Wat, Cambodia

The question is an old one,
how much to adore, how much to forget.

For three hundred years, a boy carved from wood
burnished to a luster,
kneels before the Buddha.

The boy's eyes are open, in awe.
He is an arhat, a young boy
permitted to feel the Buddha's shimmering wisdom,
the mind of one
who sits in stillness.

The boy wears a gold-flecked headpiece
and belted sampot.
The dark wood from which he is made—
koki or teak, as ephemeral
as this life,
spotted with age
and disappointment.

Near the temple where the boy
has sat for three hundred years
sugar palms show the mark of bullets
in their green wood.

We know the heart will never be finished
wanting the earth,
so we suffer.

And the mind, lonely visitor to the body,
waits for a welcome
before entering the fragrant trees of the forest.

Janet E. Aalfs

BLEEDING THE RADIATORS

Every autumn I try again
to open the valve
in one radiator that refuses

to be bled. So be it.
Let the air bubbles reign
in that region, and the rattling

at night in my head.
Let secrets hiss
through my veins. Okay. I'm still

alive. Poisoned
by desire. Enough to fuel
this house and all the houses

from here to outerspace.
If I were a plumber
I'd have the proper tools

and a logical description
of the mysteries of a system
running somewhere in these walls.

But I've come to accept
the work of one who must
time after time return

to the jammed bolt
without a clue. And to the savor
of common grit. And to aspirations

of belief in a hidden
current, joint I'll unlock someday
into the next blazing form.

The Poets

JANET E. AALFS (Northampton, MA) ▪ I've always been tall for my age, long-limbed, and able to access those pesky high shelves. Publishing *Reach* made me feel like I had 20 limbs instead of four with which to offer and receive in all directions the infinite gifts of poetry.

AMANDA AUCHTER (Houston, TX) ▪ At 20, I had not traveled far from home. A decade later, I had been to more than 20 locations, including New Orleans. My second book, *The Wishing Tomb,* is my love letter to this historical, very American city. The book is filled with the conflict between the city's dark desires and its bright musical joy.

CATHERINE ANDERSON (Kansas City, MO) ▪ At 20, I watched the wind catch the branches of an old buckeye tree and realized I wanted to write poetry the rest of my life. *The Work of Hands,* my second book, a work of ink & dreams, was published in a hinge year, the decades nested like eggs in a wren's nest ((20)00).

MELANIE BRAVERMAN (Provincetown, MA) ▪ There are at least 20 real people I name in *Red,* and all, save the dead, still talk to me. During my 20th year in Provincetown, 2002, Perugia Press made it possible for me to send the place and people I love a valentine. Thank you.

ALMITRA DAVID (1941–2003) ▪ Rochelle Toner, Almitra's partner and cover artist for her Perugia Press book, says that *Impulse to Fly* was not a reflection of Almitra's intention to fly from this life so soon, although the last poem in the book suggests more than a fleeting acquaintance with death. We wanted more, *more* than 20 years.

CAROL EDELSTEIN (Northampton, MA) ▪ When a teacher asked 20-something me if I aspired to be a famous writer, I said,

"I want to be famous with my friends." Though I often gave smart-aleck responses then, this was an answer I stand by. I'm grateful for *The Disappearing Letters,* especially because of the abiding friendships it has unexpectedly brought.

MELODY S. GEE (St. Louis, MO) ▪ At 20, my mother was a newly married immigrant in the U.S. When I was 20, she took me to see China, and so began the decade of writing *Each Crumbling House.* The book told my mother's story and let me begin telling more of my own, which today is filled with my own daughters, faith, teaching, and writing.

FAYE GEORGE (Bridgewater, MA) ▪ "You do have a thing about stones," my poet friend comments. And why not? *A Wound on Stone,* a good 20 years in the making, paved my way, and stands as the cornerstone to my life as poet.

DIANE GILLIAM (Akron, OH) ▪ The spring of 2016 marked 20 years since I walked into my first writing workshop, feeling like I was coming into a country whose language I couldn't speak. *Kettle Bottom* is still one of the most important and exciting things to happen to me in those 20 years.

JENIFER BROWNE LAWRENCE (Poulsbo, WA) ▪ When I was nine, I caught a 100-lb. halibut with 20-lb. test line. Writing *Grayling* was like that—years of effort to pull this fish from the water, not quite sure whether the fish would pull me under instead. All I knew for certain was to never let go of the pole.

FRANNIE LINDSAY (Belmont, MA) ▪ I was the 10th Perugia Press Prize winner, the halfway woman, although 10 was, and is, a benchmark. The press celebrated its birthday and my book, *Lamb,* with a standing-room-only reading. Now my fifth book is out; I'm one quarter of the way to 20. I love being a Perugia Press poet.

GAIL MARTIN (Kalamazoo, MI) ▪ It took 20 tries to find the right cover art for *Begin Empty-Handed,* an image that embodies both interior and natural worlds, the disconcerting confluence of life's gifts and its whammies. No birds were sacrificed in its creation. I love it.

LISA ALLEN ORTIZ (Santa Cruz, CA) ▪ I can do 20 push-ups and drink two shots of tequila and do zero cartwheels. (Two plus zero equals 20 if you add after the tequila.) On page 20 of *Guide to the Exhibit* is a poem that required 20 drafts and 22 emails between the editor, Susan Kan, and me.

NANCY K. PEARSON (Frederick, MD) ▪ When I was 20, I was committed to a psych ward for the first time. *Two Minutes of Light* was born there, in the halls and smoking rooms, in the bedrooms with plastic-covered mattresses in seven different cities. Words— mismatched and minute. Years of dark sleeplessness. Every line reborn.

LINDA TOMOL PENNISI (Syracuse, NY). ▪ Over and over I entered tight seams of prehistoric dark, bootlegging coal from 20 mines to haul up just the right fuel for *Seamless.* These days I can be found mining open spaces in dense woods with my grandchildren, capturing sun and wind in rinsed-out jam and pickle jars.

IDA STEWART (Haverford, PA) ▪ I've cheerfully conversed with upwards of 20 telemarketers since Susan Kan called with the good news about *Gloss* on that fateful January evening back in 2011. The caller ID said "unknown," and I thought for sure it'd be someone trying to sell me something. Since then, I always greet the unknown with a bright *hello!*

JENNIFER K. SWEENEY (Redlands, CA) ▪ *How to Live on Bread and Music* became its own good luck song. An award that brought a wider audience than I thought possible, the birth of two sons, a return to California. When I see the yellow cover bordering my father's art, I feel gratitude's hum for what grounded a life in poetry. In 20 years, I know I'll feel the same way.

GAIL THOMAS (Northampton, MA) ▪ Little did I know 20 years ago that *Finding the Bear* would be the seed that would launch the press. My writing life continued with two more books, residencies, and many readings. The Perugia Press seed—nurtured by compost, weeding, and the support of writers, readers, and other small publishers—blossomed.

LYNNE THOMPSON (Los Angeles, CA) ▪ Twenty years ago, I began writing poems for a first manuscript. Nervously, I submitted it to Perugia Press, which not only selected it for publication, but wisely edited and christened it *Beg No Pardon*. It still sells well at readings.

CORRIE WILLIAMSON (Helena, MT) ▪ It's safe to say I'd been writing poems for 20 years when *Sweet Husk* came to be. My mother still has a copy of a poem eight-year-old me wrote about clouds, written on a vaguely cloud-like piece of construction paper with a tiny dancing girl drawn in the cloud's corner. I still feel like that figure when I hold my book in my hands.

The Books

Guide to the Exhibit, Lisa Allen Ortiz (2016)
Grayling, Jenifer Browne Lawrence (2015)
Sweet Husk, Corrie Williamson (2014)
Begin Empty-Handed, Gail Martin (2013)
The Wishing Tomb, Amanda Auchter (2012)
Gloss, Ida Stewart (2011)
Each Crumbling House, Melody S. Gee (2010)
How to Live on Bread and Music, Jennifer K. Sweeney (2009)
Two Minutes of Light, Nancy K. Pearson (2008)
Beg No Pardon, Lynne Thompson (2007)
Lamb, Frannie Lindsay (2006)
The Disappearing Letters, Carol Edelstein (2005)
Kettle Bottom, Diane Gilliam (2004)
Seamless, Linda Tomol Pennisi (2003)
Red, Melanie Braverman (2002)
A Wound on Stone, Faye George (2001)
The Work of Hands, Catherine Anderson (2000)
Reach, Janet E. Aalfs (1999)
Impulse to Fly, Almitra David (1998)
Finding the Bear, Gail Thomas (1997)

This book was typeset in Arno Pro, a type family designed in 2007 by Robert Slimbach for Adobe Systems, Inc. The type, both beautiful and legible, combines classical letterforms with a warm and graceful calligraphic style. Arno was used in the production of Perugia Press's *How to Live on Bread and Music* (2009), *Each Crumbling House* (2010), and *The Wishing Tomb* (2012).